Getting the Main Point
Separating the wheat from the chaff

Walter Pauk, Ph.D.
Professor of Education
Director, Reading-Study Center
Cornell University

Jamestown Publishers
Providence, Rhode Island

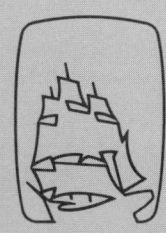

A Skill at a Time Series
No. ST-6 Getting the Main Point

ISBN 0-89061-026-6

Copyright ©1975 by Jamestown Publishers, Inc.

All rights reserved. The original material contained in this book is protected under the United States Copyright Law. It is illegal to copy or reproduce any pages or parts of any pages. Address inquiries to Editor, Jamestown Publishers, Post Office Box 6743, Providence, Rhode Island 02940.

Cover and Text Design by
Stephen R. Anthony

Printed in the United States

CONTENTS Preface 4

To Students 5

Getting the Main Point 7

A Skill at a Time Paragraphs 13

Answer Key & Recording Chart 64

PREFACE For anyone who wants to improve his basic reading skills, there is no truer, nor surer advice than: "Well, begin *reading*." Read words, signs, labels, short stories, books . . . but *read*! In other words, *practice, practice, practice.*

This is good and sufficient advice for developing the basic skills needed for reading labels and straightforward writing. But when it comes to reading mature writing, then this kind of undirected, trial-and-error practice has serious limitations.

Without directed practice, it is easy to imagine a person going through life almost totally unaware, for example, of the value of *signal words,* of the symbolic meaning of *figurative* language, of how to recognize *points of view,* and so forth. To save students from falling into such a serious "reading gap," this series of books was written.

This series of ten books is an outgrowth of notions, ideas and insights gathered over a period of more than twenty years. And during this time, many of these notions, ideas and insights were honed and polished in classes and seminars at Cornell, and thereby and therein they emerged as the ten essential categories which now form the basis for this practical and systematic program.

And now to acknowledge gladly my debts: To those students who took part in my classes and seminars, I give thanks for I learned much from them. My especial thanks goes to those students who contributed or suggested some unusually good excerpts to add to the store I already had.

In addition, I wish cordially to thank Jean Cahill of the English Department of the Providence Public Schools for her part in polishing and refining the questions.

And finally, thanks to G. Edward Lewis, Chairman, Humanities Department at Mt. Pleasant Area Senior High School in Westmoreland County, Pennsylvania, for reading all of the introductory lessons in these texts and improving them in many ways. And to all others, too numerous to mention, who have helped, I thank and am forever indebted.

                                                              Walter Pauk

Ithaca, New York
1975

TO STUDENTS   When you say, "Let me get my hands on it," you are in harmony with the number one principle of all education: *Learning by doing.* All educators know this principle, and they use it. That's why we have labs in accounting, woodworking, chemistry, and so forth.

And that's why this book was necessary. It was necessary to provide a *personal lab* so you could get your hands and mind on actual material.

But, to make this material really useful, we still needed to get *concentration* on our side. And fortunately we were able to do so. We did it by devising the one-skill-at-a-time technique.

So finally, a fully balanced program emerged. We combined a powerful principle with a powerful technique to give us a personal lab of 100 exercises. Now you will be able to focus your attention on mastering one skill before moving on to another. Your concentration will not be jarred by the mixed-question approach. You won't be forced to shift your concentration from one type of question to another.

Scanning for Author and Title   Edward Gibbon, the great historian who wrote the *Decline and Fall of the Roman Empire*, always used it. He would take a few minutes to recall what he already knew about the author and the story. Even the smallest bit of information would establish in his mind a "magnetic center" around which would cluster, like iron filings, the events of the story.

You, too, can use scanning not only for establishing magnetic centers, but also for gaining instant concentration. Once you establish a *mental set* on the story, it is difficult for outside thoughts to break in. So, with concentration and magnetic centers on your side, comprehension of a high level is bound to result.

Using the Gestalt-Dot System   *Gestalt* is a German word meaning "the whole thing." So, Gestalt psychologists would say, "Read the whole passage to get an immediate overall idea. Then go back to read each sentence more carefully. Now each sentence will be understood in relation to the whole."

To develop this concept into a useful skill, make the Gestalt sweep first, and on the basis of this first reading, answer the question by placing a dot in the square beside the option that you think is correct. This dot will indicate your unofficial answer.

Using the Check-Mark System

Now, re-read the passage, but this time indicate your official answer with a check mark (✓). This answer will count toward your final score.

The Optimum Learning Bite

The optimum learning bite is five passages. So, after every five passages, transfer your official answers to the lower portion of each block of the Answer Key Chart. The upper portion of each block already contains the correct answer. So, if your answer is correct, make no additional mark. But, if your answer is incorrect, then circle it. With your incorrect answers thus identified, take the next step.

Taking Corrective Action

Your incorrect answers provide an opportunity to continue the process of self-learning. Now that you know the correct answer, re-read the passage to see why the approved option is correct and analyze why you chose the incorrect option.

Recording Your Score

Tear out the Answer Key Chart page. Having the sheet in front of you will make it easier to record your official answers and to refer to it as your eyes check back and forth during the correction stage. Give yourself twenty points for each correct answer.

The Steps in a Nutshell

1. *Author-Title Scanning:* Spend a minute to recall what you know about both. This recall establishes powerful "magnetic centers," as well as instant concentration.
2. *The Gestalt-Dot System:* Read the passage straight through to grasp the big picture, then answer the question using the unofficial dot.
3. *The Check-Mark System:* Re-read the passage carefully. This time, put a check mark (✓) in a block to indicate your official answer.
4. *The Optimum Learning Bite:* After completing five passages, stop to check your answers.
5. *The Answer Key Chart:* Transfer your official answers to the Answer Key Chart. Circle the incorrect ones.
6. *Corrective Action:* Investigate all incorrect answers. Analyze your mistakes.
7. *Record Your Score:* Record your comprehension score.

GETTING THE MAIN POINT

Since most authors write with a purpose in mind, it is safe to suggest that most writing has a main idea. In longer works of literature, the main or controlling idea is usually referred to as the theme. Arriving at the finished story or essay is not a fast process, however. Just as a builder constructs a house one block at a time, so does an author write a story one unit at a time. His unit is the paragraph.

Perhaps the best way to learn to recognize the theme of an entire work is to practice identifying the main ideas of its member paragraphs. Whereas the main idea of an entire work is referred to by the label "theme," the main idea of a paragraph is referred to as its topic sentence.

The Topic Sentence

A good topic sentence will do two things: First, it captures our attention; and second, it motivates us to want to read on and find out the rest of the story. A topic sentence usually will contain two things also: First, an announcement of the subject or what is to come; and second, the author's attitude toward that subject. Usually it comes as the first sentence because this placement allows the author to control what follows in exact and precise terms.

We will explore the topic sentence in three types of paragraphs: expository, descriptive and narrative. Each type differs somewhat from the others according to its function and its result.

The Expository Paragraph

The most common of the paragraphs is the expository. Expository means to explain. The end result of an exposition should be new *knowledge, awareness* or *understanding.* The author wants to explain an idea or a fact so more people will comprehend it. Although this sort of technique does appear in fiction, it lends itself best to nonfiction.

Here is a paragraph from Washington Irving's *The Alhambra.* He is describing the interior of the palace that Moorish kings once lived in when they ruled in Spain. He is just about to pass into the interior from the outer courtyard in this scene.

> *The transition was almost magical.* It seemed as if we were at once transported into other times and another realm and were treading the scenes of an Arabian story. We found our-

selves in a great court paved with white marble and decorated at each end with light Moorish columns. It is called the court of the Alberca. In the center was an immense basin, or fishpool, a hundred and thirty feet in length, by thirty in breadth, stocked with gold fish and bordered by hedges of roses. At the upper end of this court rose the great tower of Comares.

Apply these questions for your own understanding:

1. Does the first sentence contain a main idea that is expanded in the rest of the paragraph? Summarize it. Did you look up the word "transition"?
2. Does the first sentence catch your attention and fire your curiosity to know more? Why was it magical?
3. What is Irving's subject in that sentence? What is his attitude toward that subject?

Sometimes an author will vary his placement of the topic sentence by placing it at the end or in the middle. Wherever the sentence occurs, apply these questions. Affirmative answers will indicate a well-thought-out topic sentence.

The Descriptive Paragraph

The descriptive paragraph is common to fiction. Its function is to describe a person, place, idea, thing or situation. Such description should result in a mental picture and usually achieves this best when it appeals to the five senses: seeing, hearing, feeling, tasting and smelling. Whereas the expository seeks to reveal new knowledge, the descriptive paragraph seeks to create an *impression*.

Here are some sample paragraphs of description. Pay particular attention to their stated or implied topic sentences and how they are supported and expanded.

Description of a Person

The first paragraph is from Stephen Crane's "Maggie: A Girl of the Streets."

When Jimmie was a little boy he began to be arrested. Before he reached a great age, he had a fair record. He developed too great a tendency to climb down from his truck and fight with other drivers. He had been in quite a number of miscellaneous fights and in some general barroom rows that had become known to the police. Once he had been arrested for assaulting a Chinaman.

Notice how he catches your attention — this fellow began to be arrested — when he was a little boy! Doesn't that make you want to know what he did and why he got arrested? His subject in this sentence is Jimmie, the little boy; his attitude: began to be arrested. The rest of the paragraph tells how and why.

Not all descriptive paragraphs have stated topic sentences, however. Since these paragraphs strive for impression, some authors plunge right into the description at the very beginning. Take Samuel Clemens's approach in the following passage from *Huckleberry Finn.*

> One of these fellows was about seventy, or upwards, and had a bald head and very grey whiskers. He had an old battered-up slouch hat on, and a greasy blue woolen shirt, and ragged old blue jeans britches stuffed into his boot tops, and home-knit galluses — no, he only had one. He had an old long-tailed blue jeans coat with slick brass buttons flung over his arm, and both of them had big fat ratty-looking carpet-bags.

In this sample, Clemens implies a sentence by the end of his description: Here is one ornery character!

Description of a Situation

The first paragraph is taken from Sherwood Anderson's "The Teacher."

> George Willard rolled about in the bed on which he had lain in the afternoon hugging the pillow and thinking thoughts of Kate Swift. The fire in the stove had gone out, and he had undressed in the cold. The sheets were like blankets of dry snow. His eyes stared about the room. The resentment, natural to the baffled male, passed and he tried to understand what had happened. He could not make it out. Over and over he turned the matter in his mind. Hours passed and he began to think it must be time for another day to come. At four o'clock he pulled the covers up about his neck and tried to sleep.

The second sample is taken from Stephen Crane's short story, "George's Mother."

> His mother was not at home. In his little room he mechanically undressed and bathed his head, arms, and shoulders. When he crawled between the two white sheets he felt a first lifting of his misery. His pillow was soothingly soft. There was an effect that was like the music of tender voices.

Can you tell which author relies on a stated topic sentence? Although these are just glimpses, can you imagine the possible situations in each? Is George Willard happy or sad? Content or confused? Satisfied or frustrated? In "George's Mother," is George's mind at ease? What is being in bed like for each of them? Just to fill you in, George Willard's teacher was tempting him sexually, but then she backed down. Crane's George has just come home from an all-night drinking party, and he is feeling poorly!

You should begin to see from these examples how authors choose words that appeal to emotions and senses when they need to describe something. Note also that even though many descriptive paragraphs will not contain stated topic sentences, the various parts and functions (subject, attitude, interest) of the topic sentence will be served by the rest of the paragraph or implied by the paragraph as a whole.

The Narrative Paragraph The narrative paragraph appears about equally often in fiction as in nonfiction. Its function is to tell something, and that something is usually a story. The story may be real or imagined, but it should contain all the features of a regular story: plot and main idea especially. A narrative paragraph often appeals to suspense also or other agents that move the narrator through a series of events or impressions.

Notice the effect that Helen Keller is able to create by relating two examples from her actual history in support of her topic sentence. The topic sentence ("Arithmetic seems to have been the only study I did not like.") and the examples are taken from her book, *The Story of My Life*.

> Arithmetic seems to have been the only study I did not like. From the first I was not interested in the science of numbers. Miss Sullivan tried to teach me to count by stringing beads in groups, and by arranging kindergarten straws I learned to add and subtract. I never had patience to arrange more than five or six groups at a time. When I accomplished this my conscience was at rest for the day, and I went out quickly to find my playmates.

Take it apart. What is the chief idea? Right, her study of arithmetic. What attitude is Keller taking toward it? Right again, she disliked it. Does this remind you of similar feelings you may have had toward one of your school subjects? Does it make you want to read on to see if she had any way of overcoming the subject or her dislike? The stage is set in that first sentence.

Now then, look at her examples. She goes back and tells another story: "Why I remember one time when I strung beads and another when I counted straws . . . ." She is telling the story of her life, its likes and dislikes, hardships and joys, but she is clever enough to insert a little incident like the beads and straws. It is a sub-story within the greater story of her life. It could be expanded into a full-scale story in its own right.

In summary, the expository paragraph explains something; the descriptive paragraph creates an impression; and the narrative paragraph tells a little story. Capturing the main ideas of individual paragraphs prepares you to grasp the theme of the whole story.

ROBINSON CRUSOE
Daniel Defoe
1

They listened always very attentively to my discourses on these heads, but especially to that part which related to the buying of Negroes, which was a trade at that time not only not far entered into, but, as far as it was, had been carried on by the *assientos,* or permission of the kings of Spain and Portugal, and engrossed in the public, so that few Negroes were bought, and those excessive dear.

The central thought of the passage is that slaves were so expensive because
☐ a. the demand for slaves exceeded the supply.
☐ b. the supply of slaves was excessive.
☐ c. a buyer had to have contacts.
☐ d. many black people refused to become slaves.

ADVENTURES OF HUCKLEBERRY FINN
Mark Twain
2

But by-and-by pap got too handy with his hick'ry, and I couldn't stand it. I was all over welts. He got to going away so much, too, and locking me in. Once he locked me in and was drowned and I wasn't ever going to get out any more. I was scared. I made up my mind I would fix up some way to leave there. I had tried to get out of that cabin many a time, but I couldn't find no way.

The two words that best help to convey the writer's main point about Huck Finn's feelings are
☐ a. lonesome and scared.
☐ b. lonesome and dreadful.
☐ c. drowned and scared.
☐ d. angry and frightened.

THE INNOCENTS ABROAD
Mark Twain
3

A little after noon on that distinguished Saturday I reached the ship and went on board. All was bustle and confusion. [I have seen that remark before somewhere.] The pier was crowded with carriages and men; passengers were arriving and hurrying on board; the vessel's decks were encumbered with trunks and valises; groups of excursionists, arrayed in unattractive traveling costumes, were moping about in a drizzling rain and looking as droopy and woebegone as so many molting chickens. The gallant flag was up, but it was under the spell, too, and hung limp and disheartened by the mast. Altogether, it was the bluest, bluest spectacle! It was a pleasure excursion—there was no gainsaying that, because the program said so—it was so nominated in the bond—but it surely hadn't the general aspect of one.

The passage is mostly about the fact that
☐ a. the trip was going to be a bore.
☐ b. he wanted to describe the ship.
☐ c. he wanted to describe the people.
☐ d. he wanted to set a scene.

MAIN TRAVELLED ROADS
Hamlin Garland
4

Rose was a large girl of twenty-five or thereabouts, and was called an old maid. She radiated good-nature from every line of her buxom self. Her black eyes were full of drollery, and she was on the best of terms with Howard at once. She had been a teacher, but that did not prevent her from assuming a peculiar directness of speech. Of course they talked about old friends.

The main point of the paragraph is that Rose
☐ a. has pretty eyes.
☐ b. is a good talker.
☐ c. seems to have a friendly personality.
☐ d. accepts being an old maid.

IN SEARCH OF ANCIENT MYSTERIES
Alan and Sally Landsburg
5

As the period of silence lengthened, more search planes went. They had no difficulty maintaining radio contact with the tower and with each other, but they saw nothing. The sky was clear and the ocean was calm.

Fishing boats and coastal steamers converged on the area. Air Force bases in Florida sent planes to help search. Since the Avenger bombers of Flight 19 could be expected to remain afloat for hours after even the most inept crash landings on the water, someone seemed certain to sight them soon. But no one did.

The main purpose of the writer is to
☐ a. amuse the reader.
☐ b. recount the details of a mysterious disappearance.
☐ c. warn others against flying over the ocean.
☐ d. explain the vanishing Avenger bombers of Flight 19.

SEVEN DAYS IN MAY
Fletcher Knebel and Charles W. Bailey II
6

Back at his desk, Casey found he still had the little wad of paper from the conference table. He unfolded it absently as he mused on Scott's mention of a possible promotion for him. By the book, he wasn't due for consideration for another three years. By then there might not be so many stars to hand out, thanks to the disarmament treaty. At least that was the way a lot of hungry colonels around here had it figured. Better not waste a lot of time thinking about it.

This passage is intended to show that Casey
☐ a. felt he deserved a promotion.
☐ b. made an exhibit of himself at the conference table.
☐ c. would not take a promotion until he deserved it.
☐ d. would not worry about a promotion at the present time.

KIDNAPPED
Robert Louis
Stevenson
7

The next time he came to see me, I was lying betwixt sleep and waking, my eyes wide open in the darkness, the sickness quite departed, but succeeded by a horrid giddiness and swimming that was almost worse to bear. I ached, besides, in every limb, and the cords that bound me seemed to be of fire. The smell of the hole in which I lay seemed to have become part of me; and during the long interval since his last visit I had suffered tortures of fear, now from the scurrying of the ship's rats, that sometimes pattered on my very face, and now from the dismal imaginings that haunt the bed of fever.

The narrator points mostly to
☐ a. the horror of being helpless in this place.
☐ b. the terrible odors of the hole.
☐ c. the agony of pain.
☐ d. the sickness and fever which go unattended.

DAVID COPPERFIELD
Charles Dickens
8

I laboured hard at my book, without allowing it to interfere with the punctual discharge of my newspaper duties; and it came out and was very successful. I was not stunned by the praise which sounded in my ears, notwithstanding that I was keenly alive to it, and thought better of my own performance, I have little doubt, than anybody else did. It has always been in my observation of human nature that a man who has any good reason to believe in himself never flourishes himself before the faces of other people in order that they may believe in him. For this reason, I retained my modesty in every self-respect; and the more praise I got, the more I tried to deserve.

The author's main point concerns the value of
☐ a. hard work.
☐ b. punctuality.
☐ c. self-confidence.
☐ d. observing human nature.

ROBINSON CRUSOE
Daniel Defoe
9

He bid me observe it, and I should always find, that the calamities of life were shared among the upper and lower part of mankind; but that the middle station had the fewest disasters, and was not exposed to so many vicissitudes as the higher or lower part of mankind; nay, they were not subjected to so many distempers and uneasinesses either of body or mind as those were who, by vicious living, luxury, and extravagances on one hand or by hard labor, want of necessaries, and mean or insufficient diet on the other hand, bring distempers upon themselves by the natural consequences of their way of living; that the middle station of life was calculated for all kind of virtues and all kinds of enjoyment....

The main idea of this paragraph is that
☐ a. only middle class people can be virtuous.
☐ b. one does not want what one never had.
☐ c. money is the solution to all woes.
☐ d. middle class life is the most care-free.

THE RED BADGE OF COURAGE
Stephen Crane
10

In a defeat there would be a roundabout vindication of himself. He thought it would prove, in a manner, that he had fled early because of his superior powers of perception. A serious prophet upon predicting a flood should be the first man to climb a tree. This would demonstrate that he was indeed a seer.

In the above passage, the author is saying that losing the battle would
☐ a. justify the man's having deserted.
☐ b. prove the man a seer.
☐ c. be the same thing as climbing a tree.
☐ d. be the first step in losing the war.

MOLL FLANDERS
Daniel Defoe
11

I was at a loss in my thoughts to conclude at first what this gentleman designed; but I found afterward he had had some drink in his head, and that he was not very unwilling to have some more. He carried me to the Spring Garden, at Knightsbridge, where we walked in the gardens, and he treated me very handsomely; but I found he drank freely. He pressed me also to drink, but I declined it.

The focus of this paragraph is on the fact that
☐ a. the man drinks quite liberally.
☐ b. the woman was concerned about her welfare.
☐ c. the woman wasn't having a good time.
☐ d. the man was acting foolishly.

KON-TIKI
Thor Heyerdahl
12

On almost every island learned men could enumerate the names of all the island's chiefs back to the time when it was first peopled. To assist their memories they often used a complicated system of knots on twisted strings, as the Inca Indians did in Peru. Modern scientists have collected all these local genealogies from different islands and found they agree with one another with astonishing exactness, both in names and number of generations. It has been discovered in this way, by taking an average Polynesian generation to represent twenty-five years, that the South Sea islands were not peopled before about 500 A. D.

The central thought of the passage is that
☐ a. the island's men are very intelligent.
☐ b. their excellent memories are attributed to a system of knots.
☐ c. it has been discovered that these islands weren't peopled before 500 A. D.
☐ d. modern scientists have found astonishing exactness in the "knot systems."

BARNABY RUDGE
Charles Dickens
13

It was on one of those mornings, common in early spring, when the year, fickle and changeable in its youth like all other created things, is undecided whether to step backward into winter or forward into summer, and in its uncertainty inclines now to the one and now to the other, and now to both at once—wooing summer in the sunshine, and lingering still with winter in the shade—it was, in short, on one of those mornings when it is hot and cold, wet and dry, bright and lowering, sad and cheerful, withering and genial, in the compass of one short hour, that old John Willet, who was dropping asleep over the copper boiler, was roused by the sound of a horse's feet, and glancing out at window, beheld a traveller, of goodly promise checking his bridle at the Maypole door.

The best statement of the main point is in
☐ a. describing the kind of day it was.
☐ b. setting the scene for the arrival of the traveller.
☐ c. showing the fickleness of spring.
☐ d. showing John Willet's business sense.

DE PROFUNDIS
Oscar Wilde
14

The prison style is absolutely and entirely wrong. I would give anything to be able to alter it when I go out. I intend to try. But there is nothing in the world so wrong but that the spirit of humanity, which is the spirit of love, the spirit of the Christ who is not in churches, may make it, if not right, at least possible to be borne without too much bitterness of heart.

The central thought of the passage is that
☐ a. prison life should be tempered by love and humanity.
☐ b. the spirit of Christ is not in churches.
☐ c. prison style is entirely wrong.
☐ d. it's impossible to change prison life.

PUDD'NHEAD WILSON
Mark Twain
15

He pulled down his window-blinds and lighted his candle. He laid off his coat and hat and began his preparations. He unlocked his trunk and got his suit of girl's clothes out from under the male attire in it, and laid it by. *Then* he blacked his face with burnt cork and put the cork in his pocket. His plan was, to slip down to his uncle's private sitting-room below, pass into the bedroom, steal the safe-key from the old gentleman's clothes, and then go back and rob the safe. He took up his candle to start. His courage and confidence were high, up to this point, but both began to waver a little, now. Suppose he should make a noise, by some accident, and get caught—say, in the act of opening the safe?

The main point of the above passage is clear by describing
☐ a. a man who robs a safe.
☐ b. a man's preparation for robbing a safe.
☐ c. a robber getting caught.
☐ d. a trick-or-treater.

A SENSE OF LIFE
A. de Saint-Exupéry
16

... The question is: What did she extract from it? What face did she put on these experiences? Is the essence of a work of art created as the structure is built that will capture it? No. The snare and the thing snared are not of the same essence. Consider the builder of cathedrals. He has used stones, and out of stones he has built silence.

The central thought that the paragraph expresses is that
☐ a. all good works take time to do.
☐ b. good may come from evil.
☐ c. the whole may be greater than its parts.
☐ d. attention to detail makes a work beautiful.

ROMEO AND JULIET
William Shakespeare
17

If I profane with my unworthiest hand
This holy shrine, the gentle fine is this:
My lips, two blushing pilgrims, ready stand
To smooth that rough touch with a tender kiss.

The main purpose of these lines is
☐ a. to express awkwardness.
☐ b. to find an excuse to kiss the girl.
☐ c. to express tenderness should he be offensive.
☐ d. to show how to get around a girl.

TYPEE
Herman Melville
18

Fruits of various kinds were likewise suspended in leafen baskets, from the tops of poles planted uprightly, and at regular intervals, along the lower two parallel rows of cumbersome drums, standing at least fifteen feet in height, and formed from the hollow trunks of large trees. Their heads were covered with shark-skins, and their barrels were elaborately carved with various quaint figures and devices. At regular intervals they were bound round by a species of sinnate of various colours, and strips of native cloth flattened upon them here and there. Behind these instruments were built slight platforms, upon which stood a number of young men who, beating drum-heads, produced those outrageous sounds which had awakened men in the morning. Every few minutes these musical performers hopped down from their elevation into the crowd below, and their places were immediately supplied by fresh recruits. Thus an incessant din was kept up that might have startled Pandemonium.

The author's main focus is in
☐ a. describing the scene.
☐ b. sharing his knowledge of the natives.
☐ c. building gradually toward a real picture of the din.
☐ d. indicating his artistic awareness.

KON-TIKI
Thor Heyerdahl
19

Where we had stranded we had only pools of water and wet patches of coral about us, and farther in lay the calm blue lagoon. The tide was going out, and we continually saw more corals sticking up out of the water round us, while the surf which thundered without interruption along the reef sank down, as it were, a floor lower. What would happen there on the narrow reef when the tide began to flow again was uncertain. We must get away.

The men realized that
☐ a. they were caught at high tide.
☐ b. they had landed safely.
☐ c. their situation was dangerous.
☐ d. the surf was more and more threatening.

THE SCARLET LETTER
Nathaniel Hawthorne
20

Pearl, accordingly, ran to the bow-window, at the farther end of the hall, and looked along the vista of a gardenwalk, carpeted with closely shaven grass, and bordered with some rude and immature attempt at shrubbery. But the proprietor appeared already to have relinquished, as hopeless, the effort to perpetuate on this side of the Atlantic, in a hard soil and amid the close struggle for subsistence, the native English taste for ornamental gardening.

The author is mainly concerned with
☐ a. Pearl's interest in gardens.
☐ b. the English taste for ornamental gardening.
☐ c. the proprietor's obvious acknowledgment that ornamental gardening didn't flourish here.
☐ d. the description of the proprietor's attempt at gardening.

CHRONICLES OF THE CONONGATE
Sir Walter Scott
21

The general, therefore, followed Lord Woodville through several rooms into a long gallery hung with pictures, which the latter pointed out to his guest, telling the names and giving some account of the personages whose portraits presented themselves in progression. General Browne was but little interested in the details which these accounts conveyed to him. They were, indeed, of the kind which are usually found in an old family gallery. Here was a Cavalier who had ruined the estate in the royal cause; there, a fine lady who had reinstated it by contracting a match with a wealthy Roundhead. There hung a gallant who had been in danger for corresponding with the exiled Court at Saint Germains; here, one had taken arms for William at the Revolution; and there, a third that had thrown his weight alternately into the scale of Whig and Tory.

The main point of this passage is centered around
☐ a. detailed descriptions of paintings.
☐ b. the petty stories which are "behind" each painting.
☐ c. the general's lack of true concern for the paintings.
☐ d. Lord Woodville's gallery of paintings.

JANE EYRE
Charlotte Brontë
22

It was the 5th of November, and a holiday. My little servant, after helping me to clean my house, was gone, well satisfied with the fee of a penny for her aid. All about me was spotless and bright—scoured floor, polished grate, and well rubbed chairs. I had also made myself neat, and had now the afternoon before me to spend as I would.

This passage is centered around
☐ a. a servant.
☐ b. the month of November.
☐ c. the events of a holiday.
☐ d. a house cleaning.

THE TALISMAN
Sir Walter Scott
23

But habit had made the endurance of this load of panoply a second nature, both to the knight and his gallant charger. Numbers, indeed, of the Western warriors who hurried to Palestine died ere they became inured to the burning climate; but there were others to whom that climate became innocent and friendly, and among this fortunate number was the solitary horseman who now traversed the border of the Dead Sea.

The main idea of the passage is contained in the statement that
☐ a. the knight and his horse were accustomed to the hot climate.
☐ b. the knight was innocent and friendly.
☐ c. Western warriors were hurrying to Palestine.
☐ d. the knight and his horse were overcome by the hot climate.

IN BLACK AND WHITE
Rudyard Kipling
24

In the long hot nights of latter April and May all the City seemed to assemble in Lalun's little white room to smoke and to talk. Shiahs of the grimmest and most uncompromising persuasion; Sufis who had lost all belief in the Prophet and retained but little in God; wandering Hindu priests passing southward on their way to the Central Indian fairs and other affairs; Pundits in black gowns, with spectacles on their noses and undigested wisdom in their insides; bearded headmen of the wards; . . .

The writer's main point is that
☐ a. it must be hot and stuffy in Lalun's.
☐ b. only important people meet in Lalun's.
☐ c. Lalun's is a meeting place for travelers.
☐ d. Lalun's is a popular spot.

FLIGHT
John Steinbeck
25

Mama Torres had three children, two undersized black ones of twelve and fourteen, Emilio and Roy, whom Mama kept fishing on the rocks below the farm when the sea was kind and when the truant officer was in some distant part of Monterey County. And there was Pepe, the tall smiling son of nineteen, a gentle affectionate boy, but very lazy. Pepe had a tallhead, pointed at the top, and from its peak, coarse black hair grew down, like a thatch all around. Over his smiling eyes Mama cut a straight bang so he could see. Pepe had sharp Indian cheekbones and an eagle nose, but his mouth was as sweet and shapely as a girl's mouth, and his chin was fragile and chiseled. He was loose and gangling, all legs and feet, and wrists, and he was very lazy. Mama thought him fine and brave, but she never told him so. She said, "Some lazy cow must have got into thy father's family, else how could I have a son like thee."

This passage is intended
☐ a. to illustrate how lazy Pepe was.
☐ b. to describe Pepe, Mama's beloved son.
☐ c. to blame Pepe's laziness on the father.
☐ d. to show how Mama avoided the truant officer.

MY DEAR DOROTHEA
George Bernard Shaw
26

By learning to decide for yourself, you will improve greatly, and will not have to be running continually to your mother when she is reading or sewing, and disturbing her with questions. You know how annoying it is to be disturbed when you are doing anything.

The main point of this selection is
☐ a. that mother enjoys reading and sewing.
☐ b. that questions are disturbing.
☐ c. to learn to make your own decisions.
☐ d. that running continually will improve you greatly.

UP FROM SLAVERY
Booker T. Washington
27

I was among the youngest of the students who were in Hampton at that time. Most of the students were men and women—some as old as forty years of age. As I now recall the scene of my first year, I do not believe that one often has the opportunity of coming into contact with three or four hundred men and women who were so tremendously in earnest as these men and women were. Every hour was occupied in study or work. Nearly all had had enough actual contact with the world to teach them the need for education.

The passage is focused on
☐ a. a student in his beginning years of study.
☐ b. a young man trying to fit in.
☐ c. the speaker in relation to the other students.
☐ d. an over-anxious student.

BLACK BOY
Richard Wright
28

I was building up in me a dream which the entire educational system of the South had been rigged to stifle. I was feeling the very thing that the state of Mississippi had spent millions of dollars to make sure that I would never feel; I was becoming aware of the thing that the Jim Crow laws had been drafted and passed to keep out of my consciousness; I was acting on impulses that southern senators in the nation's capital had striven to keep out of Negro life; I was beginning to dream the dreams that the state had said were wrong, that the schools had said were taboo.

The main idea of the above selection is that the speaker
☐ a. acts on impulses contrary to southerners.
☐ b. defies the Jim Crow laws consistently.
☐ c. resents intellectual and emotional taboos imposed on Southern Blacks.
☐ d. disobeys school rules which are detrimental to Black people.

WALDEN
Henry D. Thoreau
29

We must learn to reawaken and keep ourselves awake, not by mechanical aids, but by an infinite expectation of the dawn, which does not forsake us in our soundest sleep. I know of no more encouraging fact that the unquestionable ability of man to elevate his life by a conscious endeavor. It is something to be able to paint a particular picture, or to carve a statue, and so to make a few objects beautiful; but it is far more glorious to carve and paint the very atmosphere and medium through which we look, which morally we can do.

The main purpose of the author is
☐ a. to tell us how to awaken ourselves.
☐ b. to inform us that we don't need alarm clocks in our lives.
☐ c. to explain the art of mind control by man.
☐ d. to explain the positivism of making a conscious effort to "live."

RINGS AROUND TOMORROW
Hugh Downs
30

The word science is constantly undergoing a change of meaning. In bygone days it was practiced and associated with various skills often having nothing to do with any branch of science as we know it today. Alchemy, magic and the black arts were defined as sciences.

This passage is intended to show that
☐ a. science is alchemy, magic and the black arts.
☐ b. science has always been associated with the same skills.
☐ c. the meaning of science is constant.
☐ d. the meaning of science changes with time.

BURMA SURGEON RETURNS
Gordon S. Seagrave, M.D.
31

Soon there was another shuffling and a muttered curse that sounded like Chinese, then a fierce challenge in Chinese from Bill Brough. If Brough was taking care of them it was all right, for he was a crack shot. We breathed easily again. Minutes later Bill crawled under the tent wall. "Chinese litter bearers with a casualty," he said. "I thought they might be masquerading Japanese so I asked them where their home towns in China were. They knew their geography and their Chinese accent was all right so I let them in. The casualty was only a flesh wound and will keep till morning. I gave him plasma. We can't have lights anyways."

The writer's main thought is that
☐ a. Bill Brough is an excellent man to have in a camp.
☐ b. the Chinese casualty was not wounded severely.
☐ c. each person must look out for himself.
☐ d. mistakes of identity could be very dangerous.

BLEAK HOUSE
Charles Dickens
32

"Mr. Jarndyce," said Gridley with a rough sort of salutation, "you bear your wrongs more quietly than I can bear mine. More than that, I tell you . . . that if I took my wrongs in any other way, I should be driven mad! It is only by resenting them, and by revenging them in my mind, and by angrily demanding the justice I never get, that I am able to keep my wits together."

This passage mostly concerns Gridley. This character is able to keep his sanity by behaving
☐ a. in a fawning manner.
☐ b. with courtly airs.
☐ c. aggressively.
☐ d. like a half-wit.

ROMOLA
George Eliot
33

After that, the popular interest in the Lenten sermons had flagged a little. But this morning, when Tito entered the Piazza di Santa Croce, he found, as he expected, that the people were pouring from the church in large numbers. Instead of dispersing, many of them concentrated themselves toward a particular spot near the entrance of the Franciscan monastery, and Tito took the same direction, threading the crowd with a careless and leisurely air, but keeping careful watch on that monastic entrance, as if he expected some object of interest to issue from it.

The central thought of this passage is
- a. the interest in the Lenten sermons had flagged.
- b. the young man found the crowds as he expected.
- c. Tito wasn't sure of what was happening at the monastery.
- d. Tito acted leisurely in the crowd.

THE AMERICAN
Henry James
34

"It is absurd for me to play when you are present," said Madame de Cintre. But the next moment she went to the piano and began to strike the keys with vehemence. She played for some time, rapidly and brilliantly; when she stopped, Newman went to the piano and asked her to begin again. She shook her head, and, on his insisting, she said, "I have not been playing for you; I have been playing for myself." She went back to the window again and looked out, and shortly afterwards left the room.

The given passage is focused on
- a. Madame de Cintre's stubborness.
- b. the piano as a means of contact between the characters.
- c. Newman's love for piano music.
- d. Madame de Cintre's hesitancy to play specifically for Newman.

HOW CHILDREN FAIL
John Holt
35

The bright child is patient. He can tolerate uncertainty and failure, and will try until he gets an answer. When all his experiments fail, he can even admit to himself and others that for the time being he is not going to get an answer. This may annoy him, but he can wait. Very often, he does not want to be told how to do the problem or solve the puzzle he has struggled with, because he does not want to be cheated out of the chance to figure it out for himself in the future. Not so the dull child. He cannot stand uncertainty or failure. To him, an unanswered question is not a challenge or an opportunity but a threat.

The main emphasis of the selection is expressed in the statement that
- ☐ a. both bright and dull children like to experience failure at times.
- ☐ b. bright children usually read constantly.
- ☐ c. when a new problem is presented the bright child will be much more relaxed about it then a dull child.
- ☐ d. the dull child should get much more mathematical and science homework than the bright child.

VICTORY
Joseph Conrad
36

You have heard enough to judge for yourself. You know as much of our connection as I know myself. The people in this part of the world went by appearances, and called us friends, as far as I can remember. Appearances—what more, what better can you ask for? In fact you can't have better. You can't have anything else.

The speaker's main point is that appearances
- ☐ a. rather than reality are most important.
- ☐ b. are what one is most often judged upon.
- ☐ c. are often deceiving.
- ☐ d. are the closest one can come to reality.

GULLIVER'S TRAVELS
Jonathan Swift
37

How many innocent and excellent persons had been condemned to death or banishment, by the practising of great ministers upon the corruption of judges, and the malice of factions. How many villains had been exalted to the highest places of trust, power, dignity, and profit: how great a share in the motions and events of courts, councils, and senates might be challenged by bawds, whores, pimps, parasites, and buffoons: how low an opinion I had of human wisdom and integrity, when I was truly informed of the springs and motives of great enterprises and revolutions in the world, and of the contemptible accidents to which they owed their success.

This paragraph tries to show that
☐ a. he is happy.
☐ b. he is fed up with government.
☐ c. he is disgusted with the way his system works.
☐ d. he doesn't understand.

A LITTLE CLOUD
James Joyce
38

The child awoke and began to cry. He turned from the page and tried to hush it: but it would not be hushed. He began to rock it to and fro in his arms but its wailing cry grew keener. He rocked it faster while his eyes began to see the second stanza.

It was useless. He couldn't read. He couldn't do anything. The wailing of the child pierced the drum of his ear. It was useless, useless! He was a prisoner for life! His arms trembled with anger and suddenly bending to the child's face he shouted: "Stop!"

The main point of the author is that among people
☐ a. parenthood can be difficult.
☐ b. patience is necessary.
☐ c. commitment requires sacrifice.
☐ d. differences need understanding.

THE GUEST
Albert Camus
39

He went out and stepped forward on the terrace in front of the schoolhouse. The two men were now halfway up to the slope. He recognized the horseman to be Balducci, the old gendarme he had known for a long time. Balducci was holding at the end of a rope an Arab walking behind him with hands bound and head lowered. The gendarme waved a greeting to which Daru did not reply, lost as he was in contemplation of the Arab dressed in a faded blue jellaba, his feet in sandals but covered with socks of heavy raw wool, his head crowned with a narrow, short chèche.

The author tries to show that
☐ a. the gendarme was cruel.
☐ b. Daru concentrated on the appearance of the Arab.
☐ c. the gendarme seemed happy over his prisoner.
☐ d. Daru knew Balducci.

GREAT EXPECTATIONS
Charles Dickens
40

This morose journeyman had no liking for me. When I was small and timid, he gave me to understand that the Devil lived in a black corner of the forge, and that he knew the fiend very well: also that it was necessary to make up the fire once in seven years, with a live boy, and that I might consider myself fuel. When I became Joe's 'prentice, Orlick was perhaps confirmed in some suspicion that I should displace him; howbeit, he liked me still less. Not that he ever said anything, or did anything, openly importing hostility; I only noticed that he always beat his sparks in my direction, and that whenever I sang Old Clem, he came in out of time.

The main thought expressed in this passage is that Orlick
☐ a. disliked the other boy.
☐ b. was afraid of losing his position.
☐ c. frightened Joe's apprentice.
☐ d. had an active imagination.

A JOURNAL OF THE PLAGUE YEAR
Daniel Defoe
41

One mischief was, that if the poor people asked these mock astrologers whether there would be a plague or no, they all agreed in general to answer "Yes," for that kept up their trade. And had the people not been kept in a fright about that, the wizards would presently have been rendered useless, and their craft had been at an end. But they always talked to them of such-and-such influences of the stars, of the conjunctions of such-and-such planets, which must necessarily bring sickness and distempers, and consequently the plague. And some had the assurance to tell them the plague was begun already, which was too true, though they that said so knew nothing of the matter.

This passage is focused on showing that the wizards
☐ a. were pleased by the plague.
☐ b. were accomplished astronomers.
☐ c. helped spread the plague.
☐ d. found a business boost in the plague.

TYPEE
Herman Melville
42

In a primitive state of society, the enjoyments of life, though few and simple, are spread over a great extent, and are unalloyed; but Civilization, for every advantage she imparts, holds a hundred evil in reserve—the heart burnings, the jealousies, the social rivalries, the family dissensions, and the thousand self-inflicted discomforts of refined life, which make up in units the swelling aggregate of human misery, are unknown among these unsophisticated people.

The main point made in this paragraph is that
☐ a. a primitive state of society has only simple enjoyments.
☐ b. civilization is more negative than positive.
☐ c. primitive societies produce a purer happiness.
☐ d. unsophisticated people are less productive.

BLEAK HOUSE
Charles Dickens
43

One disagreeable result of whispering is, that it seems to evoke an atmosphere of silence, haunted by the ghosts of sound—strange cracks and tickings, the rustling of garments that have no substance in them, and the tread of dreadful feet, that would leave no mark on the sea-sand or the winter snow. So sensitive the two friends happen to be, that the air is full of these phantoms; and the two look over their shoulders by one consent, to see that the door is shut.

The writer's main point is that
☐ a. whispering creates a mood of mystery.
☐ b. whispering can be mistaken for other disagreeable sounds.
☐ c. it is best not to whisper at all.
☐ d. whispering leads to misconceptions.

A JOURNAL OF THE PLAGUE YEAR
Daniel Defoe
44

It must be confessed that though the plague was chiefly among the poor, yet were the poor the most venturous and fearless of it, and went about their employment with a sort of brutal courage; I must call it so, for it was founded neither on religion or prudence; scarce did they use any caution, but run into any business which they could get employment in, though it was the most hazardous. Such was that of tending the sick, watching houses shut up, carrying infected persons to the pest-house, and, which was still worse, carrying the dead away to their graves.

The main point of the passage indicates that the poor, who were the chief victims of the plague,
☐ a. tried to get rich quickly.
☐ b. deserved their noble fate.
☐ c. were also the least concerned.
☐ d. were very careful to avoid it.

DAVID COPPERFIELD
Charles Dickens
45

The door opened, and Agnes, gliding in, without a vestige of colour in her face, put her arm round his neck, and steadily said, "Papa, you are not well. Come with me!" He laid his head upon her shoulder, as if he were oppressed with heavy shame, and went out with her. Her eyes met mine for but an instant, yet I saw how much she knew of what had passed.

The author stresses
☐ a. the father's illness.
☐ b. the sensitivity which Agnes shows.
☐ c. the father's obedience to Agnes.
☐ d. the role of the speaker.

KON-TIKI
Thor Heyerdahl
46

We know, therefore, with absolute certainty that the original Polynesian race must at some time, willingly or unwillingly, have come drifting or sailing to these remote islands. And a closer look at the inhabitants of the South Seas shows that it can not have been very many centuries since they came. For, even if the Polynesians live scattered over an area of sea four times as large as the whole of Europe, nevertheless they have not managed to develop different languages in the different islands. It is thousands of sea miles from Hawaii in the North to New Zealand in the South, from Samoa in the West to Easter Island in the East, yet all these isolated tribes speak dialects of a common language which we have called Polynesian.

This passage emphasizes that
☐ a. there are many dialects of Polynesian.
☐ b. it has not been very many centuries since the first inhabitants arrived.
☐ c. he is uncertain whether the inhabitants came willingly or unwillingly.
☐ d. all of the isolated tribes speak dialects of a common language.

THE SCARLET LETTER
Nathaniel Hawthorne
47

This rose-bush, by a strange chance, has been kept alive in history; but whether it had merely survived out of the stern old wilderness, so long after the fall of the gigantic pines and oaks that originally overshadowed it,—or whether, as there is fair authority for believing, it had sprung up under the footsteps of the sainted Ann Hutchinson, as she entered the prison-door,—we shall not take upon us to determine.

The passage emphasizes
☐ a. the rose bush.
☐ b. how the rose bush has been kept alive.
☐ c. the sainted Ann Hutchinson.
☐ d. gigantic pines and oaks.

THE SCARLET LETTER
Nathaniel Hawthorne
48

A tendency to speculation, though it may keep woman quiet, as it does man, yet makes her sad. She discerns, it may be, such a hopeless task before her. As a first step, the whole system of society is to be torn down, and built up anew. Then, the very nature of the opposite sex, or its long hereditary habit, which has become like nature, is to be essentially modified, before woman can be allowed to assume what seems a fair and suitable position. Finally, all other difficulties being obviated, woman cannot take advantage of these preliminary reforms, until she herself shall have undergone a still mightier change; in which, perhaps, the etherial essence, wherein she has her truest life, will be found to have evaporated.

This passage illustrates
☐ a. that woman can never change in society.
☐ b. the difficult task of changing a woman's position.
☐ c. the fact that a woman's position is hereditarily determined.
☐ d. that thinking can only make a woman unhappy.

THE VIRGINIANS
William M. Thackeray
49

Lady Maria looked any age you liked. She was a fair beauty with a dazzling white and red complexion, an abundance of fair hair which flowed over her shoulders, and beautiful round arms which showed to uncommon advantage when she played at billiards with Cousin Harry. When she had to stretch across the table to make a stroke, that youth caught glimpses of a little ankle, a little cocked stocking, and a little black satin slipper with a little red heel, which filled him with unutterable rapture, and made him swear that there never was such a foot, ankle, cocked stocking, satin slipper in . . . world.

The above passage is centered around
☐ a. the youth's crush on the woman.
☐ b. the simple beauty of the female.
☐ c. a billiard game between cousins.
☐ d. an obsession with legs.

JANE EYRE
Charlotte Brontë
50

"Now I have performed the part of a good host," pursued Mr. Rochester, "put my guests into the way of amusing each other, I ought to be at liberty to attend to my own pleasure. Miss Eyre, draw your chair still a little further forward: you are yet too far back; I cannot see you without disturbing my position in this comfortable chair, which I have no mind to do."

I did as I was bid, though I would much rather have remained somewhat in the shade: but Mr. Rochester had such a direct way of giving orders, it seemed a matter of course to obey promptly.

The main thought of this passage is that Mr. Rochester was
☐ a. resented by Miss Eyre.
☐ b. confident of his abilities.
☐ c. able to get his own way.
☐ d. unreasonable in his request.

BLEAK HOUSE
Charles Dickens
51

His formal array of words might have at any other time, as it has often had, something ludicrous in it; but at this time it is serious and affecting. His noble earnestness, his fidelity, his gallant shielding of her, his generous conquest of his own wrong and his own pride for her sake, are simply honourable, manly, and true. Nothing less worthy can be seen through the lustre of such qualities in the commonest mechanic, nothing less worthy can be seen in the best-born gentleman. In such a light both aspire alike, both rise alike, both children of the dust shine equally.

The writer's main idea is that
☐ a. people often behave differently at different times.
☐ b. most men have basically the same aspirations.
☐ c. men are most honorable when not concerned about their own selfish interests.
☐ d. it is not the man's class, but his character that is most important.

BLEAK HOUSE
Charles Dickens
52

Mr. and Mrs. Snagsby are not only one bone and one flesh, but, to the neighbours' thinking, one voice too. That voice, appearing to proceed from Mrs. Snagsby alone, is heard in Cook's Court very often. Mr. Snagsby, otherwise than as he finds expression through these dulcet tones, is rarely heard.

The central focus of this paragraph is that
☐ a. Mr. Snagsby doesn't like to talk.
☐ b. Mrs. Snagsby has a sweet voice.
☐ c. Mrs. Snagsby does the talking for both.
☐ d. Mrs. Snagsby talks a lot.

BLEAK HOUSE
Charles Dickens
53

Mr. Guppy suspects everybody who enters on the occupation of a stool in Kenge and Carboy's office, of entertaining, as a matter of course, sinister designs upon him. He is clear that every such person wants to depose him. If he be ever asked how, why, when, or wherefore, he shuts up one eye and shakes his head. On the strength of these profound views, he in the most ingenious manner takes infinite pains to counterplot, when there is no plot; and plays the deepest games of chess without any adversary.

The passage illustrates that
☐ a. Mr. Guppy is suspicious of everyone.
☐ b. the other employees are plotting against Guppy.
☐ c. Mr. Guppy plays chess frequently.
☐ d. Mr. Guppy is efficient.

THE GRAPES OF WRATH
John Steinbeck
54

And while the Californians wanted many things, accumulation, social success, amusement, luxury, and a curious banking security, the new barbarians wanted only two things—land and food; and to them the two were one. And whereas the wants of the Californians were nebulous and undefined, the wants of the Okies were beside the roads, lying there to be seen and coveted: the good fields with water to be dug for, the good green fields, earth to crumble experimentally in the hand, grass to smell, oaten stalks to chew until the sharp sweetness was in the throat. A man might look at a fallow field and know, and see in his mind that his own bending back and his own straining arms would bring the cabbages into the light and the golden eating corn, the turnips and carrots.

The author's main thought is that
☐ a. Okies are barbarians in their needs.
☐ b. the Okies' wants are truly valuable.
☐ c. the land is a good source of food.
☐ d. Californians and Okies are really similar.

THE VIRGINIANS
William M. Thackeray
55

The next meal, when the family party assembled, there was not a trace of displeasure in Madame de Bernstein's countenance, and her behaviour to all the company, Harry included, was perfectly kind and cordial. She praised the cook this time, declared the fricassee was excellent, and that there were no eels anywhere like those in the Castlewood moats; would not allow that the wine was corked, or hear of such extravagance as opening a fresh bottle for a useless old woman like her.

The major point of this passage best concerns
☐ a. Madame de Bernstein's change to a very pleasant behavior.
☐ b. the people at a dinner party.
☐ c. the woman's commonly pleasant disposition.
☐ d. the meal when the family party assembled.

THE FIR TREE
Hans Christian Anderson
56

And the servant came and chopped the tree into little pieces; a whole bundle lay there: it blazed brightly under the great brewing copper, and it sighed deeply, and each sigh was like a little shot; and the children ran up and seated themselves at the fire, looked into it, and cried, "Puff! Puff!" But at each explosion, which was a deep sigh, the tree thought of a summer day in the woods, or of a winter night there, when the stars beamed; it thought of Xmas eve and of Humpty Dumpty, the only story it had ever heard or knew how to tell; and then the tree was burned.

The central idea of the paragraph is that
☐ a. the servant chopped the tree into little pieces.
☐ b. the tree burned finally or died.
☐ c. the children enjoyed the fire.
☐ d. the tree seemed alive as it burned.

LOST HORIZON
James Hilton
57

Conway looked. The view was certainly not what he had expected, if, indeed, he had expected anything. Instead of the trim, geometrically laid-out cantonments and the larger oblongs of the hangars, nothing was visible but an opaque mist veiling an immense, sun-brown desolation. The plane, though descending rapidly, was still at a height unusual for ordinary flying. Long, corrugated mountain-ridges could be picked out, perhaps a mile or so closer than the cloudier smudge of the valleys. It was typical Frontier scenery, though Conway had never viewed it before from such an altitude. It was also, which struck him as odd, nowhere that he could imagine near Peshawar. "I don't recognize this part of the world," he commented. Then more privately, for he did not wish to alarm the others, he added into Mallinson's ear: "Looks as if you're right. The man's lost his way."

The best statement of the main point is that
☐ a. the plane was landing in an unexpected place.
☐ b. Conway didn't recognize his location.
☐ c. Mallison was a perceptive person.
☐ d. Peshawar was not located on the Frontier.

TOM SAWYER ABROAD
Mark Twain
58

Nat's adventure was like this; I don't know how true it is: maybe he got it out of a paper, or somewhere, but I will say this for him, that he did know how to tell it. He could make anybody's flesh crawl, and he'd turn pale and hold his breath when he told it, and sometimes women and girls got so faint they couldn't stick it out. Well, it was this way, as near as I can remember: ....

The main point of this paragraph is that Nat
☐ a. was a good reader.
☐ b. was short of breath.
☐ c. was a great story-teller.
☐ d. was a great adventurer.

AN OUTPOST OF PROGRESS
Joseph Conrad
59

Carlier, smoking native tobacco in a short wooden pipe, would swagger up twirling his moustaches, and surveying the warriors with haughty indulgence, would say:

"Fine animals. Brought any bone? Yes? It's not too soon. Look at the muscles of that fellow—third from the end. I wouldn't care to get a punch on the nose from him. Fine arms, but legs no good below the knee. Couldn't make cavalry men of them." And after glancing down complacently at his own shanks, he always concluded "Pah! Don't they stink! You, Makola! Take that herd over to the fetish."

The passage illustrates that
☐ a. the warriors are strong but badly built.
☐ b. Carlier treats the warriors like so much cattle.
☐ c. the warriors feared Carlier.
☐ d. Carlier has had trouble with the warriors.

ROMOLA
George Eliot
60

Then she gathered her long hair together, drew it away tight from her face, bound it in a great hard knot at the back of her head, and taking a square piece of black silk, tied it in the fashion of a kerchief close across her head and under her chin; and over that she drew the cowl. She lifted the candle to the mirror. Surely her disguise would be complete to any one who had not lived very near to her. To herself she looked strangely like her brother Dino: the full oval of the cheek had only to be wasted; the eyes, already sad, had only to become a little sunken.

The main point of this passage is centered around
☐ a. the female's close resemblance to her brother when in her disguise.
☐ b. the woman disguising herself.
☐ c. the individual's attempt to avoid some people.
☐ d. the individual's attempt to mimic her brother.

CHRISTMAS BOOKS
William M. Thackeray
61

Our street, from the little nook which I occupy in it, and whence I and a fellow-lodger and friend of mine cynically observe it, presents a strange motley scene. We are in a state of transition. We are not as yet in the town, and we have left the country, where we were when I came to lodge with Mrs. Cammysole, my excellent landlady. I then took second-floor apartments at No. 17, Waddilove Street, and since, although I have never moved (having various little comforts about me), I find myself living at No. 46A, Pocklington Gardens.

The main point of the paragraph is that
☐ a. the street presents a motley scene.
☐ b. the excellent landlady is the reason they stay there.
☐ c. the lodgers live in a state of transition.
☐ d. the lodgers aren't happy with their lot.

MOLL FLANDERS
Daniel Defoe
62

Here I continued till I was between 17 and 18 years old, and here I had all the advantages of my education that could be imagined. The lady had masters home to teach her daughters to dance, and to speak French, and to write, and others to teach them music; and as I was always with them, I learned as fast as they; and though the masters were not appointed to teach me, yet I learned by imitation and inquiry all that they learned by instruction and direction; so that, in short, I learned to dance and speak French as well as any of them, and to sing much better, for I had a better voice than any of them.

The best expression of the author's main idea is that
☐ a. the narrator's education was inferior.
☐ b. the narrator took advantage of a good opportunity to learn.
☐ c. the narrator was vain and pompous.
☐ d. the narrator cheated the lady of the house.

HARRINGTON AND ORMOND
Maria Edgeworth
63

But in spite of all our zeal, noise, violence, and cabal, it was the least and the most simple child in the school who decided the election. This youngster had in secret offered to exchange a silver pencil-case for a top, or something of such inadequate value; Jacob, instead of taking advantage of the child, explained to him that his pencil-case was worth twenty tops. On the day of election, this little boy, mounted upon the top of a step-ladder, appeared over the heads of the crowd, and in a small clear voice, and with an eagerness which fixed attention, related the history of his pencil-case, and ended by hoping with all his heart that his friend Jacob, his honest Jacob, might be chosen. Jacob was elected.

The emphasis of this paragraph is best described by the word
☐ a. fate.
☐ b. perseverance.
☐ c. foolhardiness.
☐ d. intuition.

GREAT EXPECTATIONS
Charles Dickens
64

"Dear Magwitch, I must tell you, now, at last. You understand what I say?"
A gentle pressure on my hand.
"You had a child once, whom you loved and lost."
A stronger pressure on my hand.
"She lived and found powerful friends. She is living now. She is a lady and very beautiful. And I love her!"

The author focuses on the point that
☐ a. Magwitch's daughter is living.
☐ b. Magwitch is unable to speak.
☐ c. the daughter is beautiful and loved.
☐ d. Magwitch seems excited by the conversation.

THE ADVENTURES OF TOM SAWYER
Mark Twain
65

Three minutes later the old man and his sons, well armed, were up the hill, and just entering the sumac path on tiptoe, their weapons in their hands. Huck accompanied them no further. He hid behind a great boulder and fell to listening. There was a lagging, anxious silence, and then all of a sudden there was an explosion of firearms and a cry.

Huck waited for no particulars. He sprang away and sped down the hill as fast as his legs would carry him.

The main idea of this passage is that
☐ a. Huck was afraid and ran away.
☐ b. someone was hurt in the explosion.
☐ c. Huck was part of the group.
☐ d. Huck dropped out of his part in the episode.

MIDDLEMARCH
George Eliot
66

It was on a morning of May that Peter Featherstone was buried. In the prosaic neighborhood of Middlemarch, May was not always warm and sunny, and on this particular morning a chill wind was blowing the blossoms from the surrounding gardens on to the green mounds of Lowick churchyard. Swiftly-moving clouds only now and then allowed a gleam to light up any object, whether ugly or beautiful, that happened to stand within its golden shower. In the churchyard the objects were remarkably various, for there was a little country crowd waiting to see the funeral. The news had spread that it was to be a "big burying"; the old gentleman had left written directions about everything and meant to have a funeral "beyond his betters."

This passage is focused on
☐ a. funerals.
☐ b. the May weather.
☐ c. Peter's death.
☐ d. the old man's funeral.

OUR HEARTS WERE YOUNG AND GAY
Cornelia Otis Skinner and Emily Kimbrough
67

One day Mother, who had read in the *Times* that the Royal Family was to leave for the country at eleven, scuttled us off to Buckingham Palace to watch the departure. We stood along with a handful of governesses and casual passers-by . . . nobody else seemed to have made an occasion of it . . . when the gates opened and the Family appeared, rather crowded into one car like any other family starting for the station. The few men around us took off their hats, the nannies pointed out the car to their children, and Emily and I just looked. But not Mother. *Not* for nothing had she assisted on the stage the entrance of Kings and Queens. She fluttered to the ground in a deep, Eighteenth Century curtsey, spreading as wide as possible the skirt of her tailored suit. We looked down at her in amazement. We weren't the only ones amazed . . . Queen Mary nearly fell out of the car.

This passage focuses on the fact that
☐ a. few people came to say farewell to the Royal Family.
☐ b. the Queen was amused at mother's actions.
☐ c. the Royal Family deserved a holiday.
☐ d. mother knew how to curtsey because she'd been an actress.

SCENES OF CLERICAL LIFE
George Eliot
68

"If you please 'm," the shepherd says, "have you heard as Mrs. Barton's wuss, and not expected to live?"

Mrs. Hackit turned pale, and hurried out to question the shepherd, who, she found, had heard the sad news at an alehouse in the village. Mr. Hackit followed her out and said, "You'd better have the pony-chaise, and go directly."

The best statement of the main point is that
☐ a. Mrs. Hackit was disturbed by the shepherd's news.
☐ b. the village alehouse was the source of news.
☐ c. Mrs. Barton's health had worsened.
☐ d. Mr. Hackit told his wife to help.

TEARS AND LAUGHTER
Kahil Gibran
69

He was breathing his last and had no one at his bedside save the oil lamp, his only companion, and some parchments upon which he had inscribed his heart's feeling. As he salvaged the remnants of his withering strength he lifted his hands heavenward; he moved his eyes hopelessly, as if wanting to penetrate the ceiling in order to see the stars from behind the veil of clouds.

The focus of the paragraph is in describing
☐ a. a weary soldier.
☐ b. a dying man.
☐ c. an intoxicated man.
☐ d. a dozing man.

MOLL FLANDERS
Daniel Defoe
70

The pen employed in finishing her story, and making it what you now see it to be, has had no little difficulty to put it into a dress fit to be seen, and to make it speak language fit to be read. When a woman debauched from her youth, nay, even being the offspring of debauchery and vice, comes to give an account of all her vicious practices, and even to descend to the particular occasions and circumstances, by which she first became wicked, and of all the progression of crime, which she ran through in threescore years, an author must be hard put to it to wrap it up so clean as not to give room, especially for vicious readers, to turn it to his disadvantage.

The central thought of this paragraph is that
☐ a. the material for the story was questionable.
☐ b. readers of such books are very critical.
☐ c. the author had to work at making the story presentable.
☐ d. the author was thinking of his own reputation.

47

HARD TIMES
Charles Dickens
71

It was a town of red brick, or of brick that would have been red if the smoke and ashes had allowed it; but as matters stood it was a town of unnatural red and black like the painted face of a savage. It was a town of machinery and tall chimneys, out of which interminable serpents of smoke trailed themselves for ever and ever, and never got uncoiled. It had a black canal in it, and a river that ran purple with ill-smelling dye, and vast piles of building full of windows where there was a rattling and a trembling all day long, and where the piston of the steam-engine worked monotonously up and down like the head of an elephant in a state of melancholy madness.

The main point of this paragraph is that
☐ a. the town is a business area.
☐ b. the town's been polluted by industry.
☐ c. the town is unappealing.
☐ d. it's not likely that the town will survive.

COUNTERPARTS
James Joyce
72

He felt his great body aching for the comfort of the publichouse. The fog had begun to chill him and he wondered could he touch Pat in O'Neill's. He could not touch him for more than a bob—and a bob was no use. Yet he must get money somewhere or other: he had spent his last penny for the g.p. and soon it would be too late for getting money anywhere. Suddenly, as he was fingering his watch-chain, he thought of Terry Kelly's pawn-office in Fleet Street. That was the dart! Why didn't he think of it sooner?

This passage centers around the fact that
☐ a. he was chilled and wanted a drink.
☐ b. he needed money for the drink.
☐ c. he didn't have any friends who'd lend him money.
☐ d. he could pawn his watch.

JANE EYRE
Charlotte Brontë
73

My home, then,—when I at last find a home, is a cottage: a little room with white-washed walls, and a sanded floor, containing four painted chairs and a table, a clock, a cupboard, with two or three plates and dishes, and a set of tea-things in delf. Above, a chamber of the same dimensions as the kitchen, with a deal bedstead, and chest of drawers; small, yet too large to be filled with my scanty wardrobe: though the kindness of my gentle and generous friends has increased that, by a modest stock of such things as are necessary.

The central point of the above passage is to
- a. describe a home being paid for.
- b. describe a dream home.
- c. describe the speaker's home.
- d. describe how to decorate.

THE VIRGINIANS
William M. Thackeray
74

A soft hand is held out after this pretty speech, a pair of very well-preserved blue eyes look exceedingly friendly. Harry grasps his cousin's hand with ardour. I do not know what privilege of cousinship he would not like to claim, only he is so timid. They call the English selfish and cold. He at first thought his relatives were so: but how mistaken he was! How kind and affectionate they are, especially the Earl, and dear dear Maria! How he wishes he could recall that letter which he had written to Mrs. Mountain and his mother, in which he hinted that his welcome had been a cold one!

The main point of the passage is that
- a. Harry rashly judged the kind of people his relatives were.
- b. the English are usually cold.
- c. a pretty girl can change the mind.
- d. Harry displays fickle qualities.

A FAREWELL TO ARMS
Ernest Hemingway
75

I left them working, the car looking disgraced and empty with the engine open and parts spread on the work bench, and went in under the shed and looked at each of the cars. They were moderately clean, a few freshly washed, the others dusty. I looked at the tires carefully, looking for cuts or stone bruises. Everything seemed in good condition. It evidently made no difference whether I was there to look after things or not. I had imagined that the condition of the cars, whether or not things were obtainable, the smooth functioning of the business of removing wounded and sick from dressing stations, hauling them back from the mountains to the clearing station and then distributing them to the hospitals named on their papers, depended to a considerable extent on myself. Evidently it did not matter whether I was there or not.

The author makes the point here that within an organization individuals are
☐ a. workers.
☐ b. dispensable.
☐ c. bonuses.
☐ d. necessary.

THE OLD MAN AND THE SEA
Ernest Hemingway
76

Then he was sorry for the great fish that had nothing to eat and his determination to kill him never relaxed in his sorrow for him. How many people will he feed, he thought. But are they worthy to eat him? No, of course not. There is no one worthy of eating him from the manner of his behavior and his great dignity.

The author's main point is that
☐ a. the man and fish share a fraternity.
☐ b. drones should not benefit from the work of others.
☐ c. the fish exhibits human qualities of a high order.
☐ d. nobility should not be debased.

VICTORY
Joseph Conrad
77

Schomberg felt desperation, that lamentable substitute for courage, ooze out of him. It was not so much the threat of death as the weirdly circumstantial manner of its declaration which affected him. A mere "I'll murder you," however ferocious in tone and earnest in purpose, he could have faced; but before this novel mode of speech and procedure, his imagination being very sensitive to the unusual, he collapsed as if indeed his mortal neck had been broken—snap!

The strongest focus of this passage is on Schomberg's extreme fear which is caused by
☐ a. a loss of courage.
☐ b. a physical weakness.
☐ c. a threat to his life.
☐ d. the nature of the threat.

BLEAK HOUSE
Charles Dickens
78

During the whole time consumed in the slow growth of this family tree, the house of Smallweed, always early to go out and late to marry, has strengthened itself in its practical character, has discarded all amusements, discountenanced all story-books, fairy tales, fictions, and fables, and banished all levities whatsoever. Hence the gratifying fact, that it has no child born to it, and that the complete little men and women whom it has produced, have been observed to bear a likeness to old monkeys with something depressing on their minds.

The writer's central idea is that the Smallweeds
☐ a. are a rather uncouth and unhappy family.
☐ b. have stressed practicality to the detriment of their children.
☐ c. are a very strong family because they have avoided frivolous pursuits.
☐ d. have always produced children who mature very early.

DEATH IN VENICE
Thomas Mann
79

Aschenback's whole soul, from the beginning, was bent on fame—and thus while not precisely precocious, yet thanks to the unmistakable trenchancy of his personal accent, he was early ripe and ready for a career. Almost before he was out of high school he had a name. Ten years later he had learned to sit at his desk and sustain and live up to his growing reputation, to write gracious and pregnant phrases in letters that must needs be brief, for many claims press upon the solid and successful man. At forty, worn down by the strains and stresses of his actual task, he had to deal with a daily post heavy with tributes from his own and foreign countries.

The main point of this passage is that Aschenback
☐ a. gained a reputation while still quite young.
☐ b. had little genuine talent.
☐ c. deliberately created his success.
☐ d. was a tremendously important man.

ON THE LIFE OF MAN
Sir Walter Raleigh
80

What is our life? a play of passion;
Our mirth the music of division;
Our mothers' wombs the tiring-houses be
Where we are dressed for this short comedy.
Heaven the judicious sharp spectator is,
That sits and marks still who doth act amiss;
Our graves that hide us from the searching sun
Are like drawn curtains when the play is done.
Thus march we, playing, to our latest rest,
Only we die in earnest—that's no jest.

The main point of the poem is that
☐ a. life is meaningless; death is meaningful.
☐ b. live any way you choose since death is the same for all.
☐ c. life may be compared to an actor's role in a play; death frees one from playacting.
☐ d. wise men know that life is nothing but a tragedy.

A FAREWELL TO ARMS
Ernest Hemingway
81

War is not won by victory. What if we take San Gabriele? What if we take the Carso and Monfalcone and Trieste? What are we then? Did you see all of the far mountains today? Do you think we could take all of them too? Only if the Austrians stop fighting. One side must stop fighting. Why don't we stop fighting? If they came down into Italy they would soon get tired and go away. They have their own country. But no, instead there is a war.

The author's main point is that
☐ a. war requires two aggressors.
☐ b. conflicts are not solved by further conflicts.
☐ c. wars are no longer fought to annex new lands.
☐ d. sometimes there is no alternative to conflict.

THE LOTTERY
Shirley Jackson
82

Old Man Warner snorted. "Pack of crazy fools," he said. "Listening to the young folks, nothing's good enough for *them*. Next thing you know, they'll be wanting to go back to living in caves, nobody work anymore, live *that* way for a while. Used to be a saying, 'Lottery in June, corn be heavy soon.' First thing you know, we'd all be eating stewed chickweed and acorns. There's *always* been a lottery," he added petulantly. "Bad enough to see young Joe Summers up there joking with everybody."

"Some places have already quit lotteries," Mrs. Adams said.

"Nothing but trouble in *that*," Old Man Warner said stoutly. "Pack of young fools."

The important point in Old Man Warner's attitude is that
☐ a. young people lack the wisdom of old age.
☐ b. traditional ways of doing things should not be changed.
☐ c. old men are wise and should be held in esteem.
☐ d. just because someone does something, other people do not have to follow.

SISTER CARRIE
Theodore Dreiser
83

People in general attach too much importance to words. They are under the illusion that talking effects great results. As a matter of fact, words are, as a rule, the shallowest portion of all the argument. They but dimly represent the great surging feelings and desires which lie behind. When the distraction of the tongue is removed, the heart listens.

The central thought is that
☐ a. deep feelings and desires are beyond description.
☐ b. people should talk less and listen more.
☐ c. people communicate best with their emotions and feelings.
☐ d. people do not know how to communicate with words.

ANTIGONE
Sophocles
84

Fortunate they whose lives have no taste of pain. For those whose house is shaken by the gods escape no kind of doom. It extends to all the kin like the wave that comes when the winds of Thrace run over the dark of the sea.
The black sand of the bottom is brought from the depth; the beaten capes sound back with a hollow cry.

The speaker's main point is that
☐ a. the gods are capable of inflicting numerous types of pain.
☐ b. those who have never tasted pain are rare.
☐ c. no one can escape the wrath of an angry god.
☐ d. misfortune, once begun, seems to multiply.

HELEN
Maria Edgeworth
85

There were plans to be made of all the alterations and improvements at Old Forest. Beauclerc applied to Lady Cecilia for her advice and assistance. Her advice she gave, but her assistance she ingeniously contrived to leave to Helen; for whenever Beauclerc brought to her a sketch or a plan of what was to be done, Lady Cecilia immediately gave it to Helen, repeating, "Never drew a regular plan in my life, you know, my dear, you must do this;" so that Helen's pencil and her patience were in constant requisition. Then came apologies from Beauclerc, and regrets at taking up her time, all which led to an intimacy that Lady Cecilia took care to keep up by frequent visits to Old Forest, so that Helen was necessarily joined in all his present pursuits.

The greatest concern of the author is that
☐ a. Beauclerc fancies Lady Cecilia.
☐ b. Lady Cecilia is trying to "acquaint" Beauclerc and Helen.
☐ c. Lady Cecilia is a terrible artist.
☐ d. Helen draws better than Beauclerc.

CANDIDE
Voltaire
86

When the two sight-seers had taken leave of His Excellency, Candide said to Martin: "Well now, you will agree that there is the happiest of all men; for he is above everything he possesses."

"Don't you see," said Martin, "that he is disgusted with everything he possesses? Plato said a long time ago that the best stomachs are not those which refuse all food."

The writer's central thought is that
☐ a. a happy man is able to find pleasure in something.
☐ b. a man's happiness cannot be judged by his possessions.
☐ c. a happy man is one who can be easily satisfied.
☐ d. man's happiness lies in understanding his own limitations.

DEATH IN VENICE
Thomas Mann
87

It was an ancient hulk belonging to an Italian line, obsolete, dingy, grimed with soot. A dirty hunch-backed sailor, smirkingly polite, conducted him at once belowships to a cavernous, lamplit cabin. There behind a table sat a man with a beard like a goat's; he had his hat on the back of his head, a cigar-stump in the corner of his mouth; he reminded Aschenbach of an old-fashioned circus-director. This person put the usual questions and wrote out a ticket to Venice, which he issued to the traveller with many commercial flourishes.

The emphasis in this passage is on the
☐ a. ancient hulk.
☐ b. peculiar man.
☐ c. time of day.
☐ d. atmosphere in which the characters move.

THE DEAD
James Joyce
88

"Ladies and Gentlemen,
I will not attempt to play tonight the part that Paris played on another occasion. I will not attempt to choose between them. The task would be an invidious one and one beyond my poor powers. For when I view them in turn, whether it be our chief hostess herself, whose good heart, whose too good heart, has become a byword with all who know her, or her sister, who seems to be gifted with perennial youth and whose singing must have been a surprise and a revelation to us all tonight, or, last but not least, when I consider our youngest hostess, talented, cheerful, hard-working and the best of nieces, I confess, Ladies and Gentlemen, that I do not know to which of them I should award the prize."

The main idea of the paragraph is that
☐ a. the speaker is careful of his words.
☐ b. one sister has more talent than the others.
☐ c. the speaker is flattering each sister equally.
☐ d. the speaker is laughing on the inside.

WASHINGTON SQUARE
Henry James
89

His first child, a little boy of extraordinary promise, as the Doctor, who was not addicted to easy enthusiasm, firmly believed, died at three years of age, in spite of everything that the mother's tenderness and the father's science could invent to save him. Two years later Mrs. Sloper gave birth to a second infant—an infant of a sex which rendered the poor child, to the Doctor's sense, an inadequate substitute for his lamented first-born, of whom he had promised himself to make an admirable man. The little girl was a disappointment; but this was not the worst. A week after her birth the young mother, who, as the phrase is, had been doing well, suddenly betrayed alarming symptoms, and before another week had elapsed, Austin Sloper was a widower.

The paragraph's main purpose is to
☐ a. recount events.
☐ b. compare feelings.
☐ c. explain the birth of children to a reader.
☐ d. amuse the reader.

VICTORY
Joseph Conrad
90

He [Schomberg] winked with immense malice. A bell started ringing, and he led the way to the dining-room as if into a temple, very grave, with the air of a benefactor of mankind. His ambition was to feed it at a profitable price, and his delight was to talk of it behind its back. It was very characteristic of him to gloat over the idea of Heyst having nothing decent to eat.

The writer's main point is to
☐ a. show the organization of the dining room.
☐ b. zero in on Schomberg's maliciousness.
☐ c. concentrate on Schomberg's efficiency.
☐ d. show the amiability of the situation.

AN OUTPOST OF PROGRESS
Joseph Conrad
91

At times Gobila came to see them. Gobila was the chief of the neighboring villages. He was a gray-headed savage, thin and black, with a white cloth round his loins and a mangy panther skin hanging over his back. He came up with long strides of his skeleton legs, swinging a staff as tall as himself, and, entering the common room of the station, would squat on his heels to the left of the door. There he sat, watching Kayerts, and now and then making a speech which the other did not understand. Kayerts, without interrupting his occupation, would from time to time say in a friendly manner: "How goes it, you old image?" and they would smile at one another. The two whites had a liking for that old and incomprehensible creature, and called him Father Gobila.

The main point of this paragraph is that
☐ a. Gobila was chief of the neighboring villages.
☐ b. there was no way of communicating with Gobila.
☐ c. the two whites liked Father Gobila.
☐ d. Gobila's being a savage made him unpredictable.

BLEAK HOUSE
Charles Dickens
92

Like a dingy London bird among the birds at roost in these pleasant fields, where the sheep are all made into parchment, the goats into wigs, and the pasture into chaff, the lawyer, smoke-dried and faded, dwelling among mankind but not consorting with them, aged without experience of genial youth, and so long used to make his cramped nest in holes and corners of human nature that he has forgotten its broader and better range, comes sauntering home.

The author stresses as his main point
☐ a. the lawyer's lack of understanding.
☐ b. the lawyer's faded life style.
☐ c. the kinds of people lawyers deal with.
☐ d. ecological problems.

THE ATHEIST'S MASS
Honore de Balzac
93

The fame of a surgeon is like the fame of an actor; it exists only as long as they live, and their talent is no longer appreciable after they have disappeared. Actors and surgeons, like great singers also, and those masters who increase the power of music tenfold by their execution, are all heroes of the moment.

The passage illustrates
☐ a. the fact that nothing survives.
☐ b. the attitude of an envious person.
☐ c. what professions should be avoided.
☐ d. how quickly our talents are forgotten.

ARABY
James Joyce
94

Her image accompanied me even in places the most hostile to romance. On Saturday evenings when my aunt went marketing I had to go to carry some of the parcels. We walked along the flaring streets, jostled by drunken men and bargaining women, amid the curses of labourers, the shrill litanies of shop-boys who stood on guard by the barrels of pigs' cheeks, the nasal chanting of street-singers, who sang a come-all-you about O'Donovan Rossa, or a ballad about the troubles in our native land. These noises converged in a single sensation of life for me: I imagined that I bore my chalice safely through a throng of foes.

The central thought of the above passage is that
☐ a. there was a chalice in one of the parcels.
☐ b. the girl's image is his chalice which he safely carried.
☐ c. the market place was rather dangerous.
☐ d. the noises caused a great deal of aggravation.

ABSALOM, ABSALOM
William Faulkner
95

It's just incredible. It just does not explain. Or perhaps that's it: they don't explain and we are not supposed to know. We have a few old mouth-to-mouth tales; we exhume from old trunks and boxes and drawers letters without salutations or signature, in which men and women who once lived and breathed are now merely initials or nicknames out of some incomprehensible affection which sound to us like Sanskrit or Chocktaw; we see dimly people in whose living blood and seed we ourselves lay dormant and waiting, ...

The author's main point is that
☐ a. life is incredible.
☐ b. we can learn from the past.
☐ c. no one can really know the past.
☐ d. letters and tales are valuable to history.

ANTIGONE
Sophocles
96

A man, though wise, should never be ashamed
of learning more, and must unbend his mind.
Have you not seen the trees beside the torrent,
the ones that bend them saving every leaf,
while the resistant perish root and branch?
And so the ship that will not slacken sail,
the sheet drawn tight, unyielding, overturns.
She ends the voyage with her keel on top.

The speaker's prime thought is that
☐ a. no matter how resistant to change man must eventually submit to it.
☐ b. natural forces change upon man.
☐ c. those who cannot accept change must suffer because of it.
☐ d. a true wise man is never insensitive to change.

JANE EYRE
Charlotte Brontë
97

It is in vain to say human beings ought to be satisfied with tranquillity; they must have action; and they will make it if they cannot find it. Millions are condemned to a stiller dome than mine, and millions are in silent revolt against their lot. Nobody knows how many rebellions besides political rebellions ferment in the masses of life which people earth. Women are supposed to be very calm generally; but women feel just as men feel; they need exercise for their faculties, and a field for their efforts as much as their brothers do.

The central idea of the above paragraph is that
☐ a. women are equal to men.
☐ b. people ought to be satisfied with tranquillity.
☐ c. men like action more than women do.
☐ d. people need to be challenged and active.

THE SCARLET LETTER
Nathaniel Hawthorne
98

The young woman was tall, with a figure of perfect elegance, on a large scale. She had dark and abundant hair, so glossy that it threw off the sunshine with a gleam, and a face which, besides being beautiful from regularity of feature and richness of complexion, had the impressiveness belonging to a marked brow and deep black eyes. She was lady-like, too, after the manner of the feminine gentility of those days; characterized by a certain state and dignity, rather than by the delicate, evanescent, and indescribable grace, which is now recognized as its indication.

The author's purpose in writing this paragraph is to
☐ a. describe her emotions.
☐ b. compliment her.
☐ c. paint a word picture of her.
☐ d. demonstrate his meticulous observations.

CRIME AND PUNISHMENT
Fyodor M. Dostoevsky
99

He glanced at her, and immediately it appeared to him, he recognized Lizaveta in her face. He vividly remembered the expression of Lizaveta's face as he approached her with the axe and she kept receding to the wall, with outstretched hand, and perfectly childish expression of fear in her face, precisely as little children do who, when they suddenly become frightened at something, immovably and restlessly look at the object of their fear, step back and begin to cry, while stretching out their little hands. Almost the same took place with Sonya.

This passage illustrates
☐ a. the sadistic tendencies which the aggressor shows.
☐ b. the precise detail with which he recalls Lizaveta's face.
☐ c. the fate of Sonya.
☐ d. the uncertainty of the aggressor's final acts.

SISTER CARRIE
Theodore Dreiser
100

The dullest specimen of humanity, when drawn by desire toward evil, is recalled by a sense of right, which is proportionate in power and strength to his evil tendency. We must remember that it may not be a knowledge of right, for no knowledge of right is predicted of the animal's instinctive recoil at evil. Men are still led by instinct before they are regulated by knowledge. It is instinct which recalls the criminal—it is instinct (where highly organized reasoning is absent) which gives the criminal his feeling of danger, his fear of wrong.

This passage illustrates that
☐ a. instinct is superior to knowledge.
☐ b. all men are basically good.
☐ c. man is instinctively repelled by evil.
☐ d. all men instinctively know the difference between right and wrong.

ACKNOWLEDGMENTS Acknowledgment is gratefully made to the following publishers for permission to reprint the works of the many authors appearing in this series: To Harper & Row for permission to reprint passages by E. B. White, Richard Wright, Fletcher Knebel, Charles W. Bailey, Edward Streeter, and George Plimpton. To Random House for permission to reprint passages by William Styron, David Halberstam, Loren Eisely, Clifford Odets, and William Faulkner. To Harcourt Brace Jovanovich, Inc., for permission to reprint passages by C. F. Ramuz, George Orwell, Katherine Anne Porter, and Milovan Djilas. To Doubleday and Co., Inc., for permission to reprint passages by Melba Marlett, Hugh Downs, Leon Uris, Wyn Sargent, and J. F. Powers. To Little, Brown and Company for permission to reprint passages by Alastair Reid, Evelyn Waugh, Walter D. Edmonds, and Erich Maria Remarque. To Dodd, Mead & Company for permission to reprint passages by Cornelia Otis Skinner and Emily Kimbrough. To W. W. Norton & Company, Inc., for permission to reprint passages by Gordon S. Seagrove, M.D. To J. B. Lippincott Company for permission to reprint passages by Leslie A. Fiedler, Harper Lee, and Louis DeWohl. To Holt, Rinehart and Winston, Inc., for permission to reprint passages by Hannah Green and Philip Roth. To St. Martin's Press, Inc., for permission to reprint passages by James Herriot. To Charles Scribner's Sons for permission to reprint passages by F. Scott Fitzgerald and Dorothy Salisburgh Davis. To Century House, Inc., for permission to reprint passages by Percy Marks. To Scarecrow Press, Inc., for permission to reprint passages by Perry D. Westbrook. To Alfred A. Knopf, Inc., for permission to reprint passages by Elizabeth Brown and Katherine Mansfield. To Coward, McCann & Geoghegan, Inc., for permission to reprint passages by Bernard Kops. To The Viking Press, Inc., for permission to reprint passages by Patrich White. To Simon & Shuster, Inc., for permission to reprint passages by Mortimer Adler and P. G. Wodehouse. To Crown Publishers, Inc., for permission to reprint passages by Brainard Cheney. To The Dial Press for permission to reprint passages by Frank Yerby. To Farrar, Straus & Giroux, Inc., for permission to reprint passages by Shirley Jackson. To Houghton, Mifflin Company for permission to reprint passages by James Dickey and Ruth Benedict. To Oxford University Press, Inc., for permission to reprint passages by Aldo Leopold. To The John Day Company, Inc., for permission to reprint passages by Pearl S. Buck. To Berkley Publishing Corporation for permission to reprint passages by Theodore L. Thomas and Kate Wilhelm. To Pocket Books for permission to reprint passages by Benjamin Spock, M.D. To Rand McNally & Company for permission to reprint passages by Thor Heyerdahl. To The Viking Press, Inc., for permission to reprint passages by John Steinbeck and Muriel Spark. To E. P. Dutton Co., Inc., for permission to reprint passages by Dick Gregory and Alexander Solzhenitsyn. To The New American Library, Inc., for permission to reprint passages by Arthur Clarke. To Pitman Publishing Corp., for permission to reprint passages by John Holt. To World Publishing Company for permission to reprint passages by Kurt Steel. The story of the origin of the word "tantalize" is reprinted by permission from *Picturesque Word Origins*, copyright 1933 by G. & C. Merriam Co., publishers of the Merriam-Webster Dictionaries.

COMBINED ANSWER KEY AND RECORDING CHART

#	Ans	#	Ans	#	Ans	#	Ans	#	Ans
1	a	2	a	3	d	4	c	5	b
6	d	7	a	8	c	9	d	10	a
11	a	12	c	13	b	14	a	15	b
16	c	17	c	18	c	19	c	20	c
21	c	22	c	23	a	24	d	25	b

Score _____ %

#	Ans	#	Ans	#	Ans	#	Ans	#	Ans
26	c	27	c	28	c	29	d	30	d
31	a	32	c	33	c	34	d	35	c
36	d	37	c	38	b	39	a	40	a
41	d	42	c	43	a	44	c	45	b
46	b	47	a	48	b	49	b	50	c

Score _____ %

#	Ans	#	Ans	#	Ans	#	Ans	#	Ans
51	d	52	a	53	b	54	a	55	a
56	b	57	a	58	c	59	b	60	b
61	c	62	b	63	b	64	a	65	a
66	d	67	d	68	c	69	b	70	c
71	b	72	b	73	b	74	a	75	b

Score _____ %

#	Ans	#	Ans	#	Ans	#	Ans	#	Ans
76	d	77	d	78	b	79	c	80	c
81	a	82	b	83	c	84	d	85	b
86	a	87	c	88	a	89	a	90	b
91	c	92	b	93	d	94	b	95	c
96	c	97	d	98	c	99	b	100	c

Score _____ %